MW01248529

What My Hands Reveal

Aren McCartney

What My Hands Reveal

Olympia Publishers
London

www.olympiapublishers.com
OLYMPIA PAPERBACK EDITION

Copyright © Aren McCartney 2023

The right of Aren McCartney to be identified as author of
this work has been asserted in accordance with sections 77 and 78 of the Copyright,
Designs and Patents Act 1988.

All Rights Reserved

No reproduction, copy or transmission of this publication
may be made without written permission.
No paragraph of this publication may be reproduced,
copied or transmitted save with the written permission of the publisher, or in
accordance with the provisions
of the Copyright Act 1956 (as amended).

Any person who commits any unauthorised act in relation to
this publication may be liable to criminal
prosecution and civil claims for damage.

A CIP catalogue record for this title is
available from the British Library.

ISBN: 978-1-80439-062-7

This is a work of fiction.
Names, characters, places and incidents originate from the writer's imagination. Any
resemblance to actual persons, living or dead, is purely coincidental.

First Published in 2023

Olympia Publishers
Tallis House
2 Tallis Street
London
EC4Y 0AB

Printed in Great Britain

Dedication

This book is dedicated to the LGBTQ+ kids around the world: keep loving, keep dreaming, keep going

Acknowledgements

I want to thank my mom and dad, who have always supported me and shown me unconditional love from the beginning. And my brother, David, who always inspires me, makes me laugh, and will always be the first friend I ever had. I love the three of you with all my heart. To my friends – Daniel, Sean, Hannah, and Kara – thank you for seeing me for who I am and helping me grow alongside you. I love each of you so much. To Lauren, who gives me the space to contemplate life and all its intricacies and helps me find myself; I'm not sure I can thank you enough. And to my twelve-year-old self, I owe it all to you: you started writing and never looked back. My full heart beats swiftly thanks to all of you.

TABLE OF CONTENTS

If the pen is mightier than the sword
Am I cutting myself too deep
Are the intrusive thoughts enough to keep me from sleep
Is the reaction physical with blood
That will be used for ink
Or is it all in my head
Mentally constraining as it guides what I think
Is my dagger too sharp, pointed at my heart

If the pen is mightier than the sword
Am I cutting myself too deep
Are the intrusive thoughts going to haunt my dreams
Will the ink be made with blood
A thick, dark red
All these feelings from deep within
Move from my heart to my head
My dagger opens up my chest, does it know what's best

If the pen is mightier than the sword
Am I cutting myself too deep
Will the ink change from black to red
And leave enough for me to keep
Everything I think I know
Seeps out onto plain paper
Marking it so deeply no white will show
My dagger stays in the middle, containing only riddles

This little dagger I hold in my fingers
When used with precision
can be such a killer
Introspection without discretion
Trying to answer all my questions
I look down to see what my hands reveal
The expression of things I feel to be real

Outside

All these words I write
That leak out of my mind
And live outside of time
Are written in deep red
From my heart to my head
Question being said
Mostly kept to myself
Is it good for my health
If only down thoughts
Measured wealth
Rarely ever shown
How well is it known
This viscous dark red tone
Insides get turned out
Attempt to decipher what
they're about
The urge to rip it out
and scream aloud
Why are they there
Is it enough to care
Seem to float through the air
Keep my head in the clouds
Drown myself underneath sounds
How long can I go in these rounds
What I am to do
Who can I turn to
Have to see it all the way through
Hope to know

Can't let this go
We'll go toe to toe
For as long as I live
I'll give and give
Until I am unresponsive

Self Talk

Does talking to myself count
as interaction
It begs the question
and I think I should mention
that these conversations
are not one-sided
and take place not
just in my head
but out in the open instead
My vocal chords vibrate
With my hands I gesticulate
and what I in turn create
is something I'm not
entirely sure has a name
But I have a name
So it's my pleasure
to introduce me to myself
And together we share
a wealth
of knowledge
Perhaps we can do our best
to figure out
at least in some small
way what this is all about
and keep each other
from giving out
So I'll keep talking to myself
For the sake of my

ever-fluctuating mental health
as I try to not be
over or underwhelmed
Maybe one day
another will join
in communication
but until that happens
I'll just start talking
to me again

Every Night

Every night
when I lay me down
I dive headfirst
into a deep black ocean
Underneath waves and turbulent
commotion,
propulsion
from the moon
The jellyfish bloom
And if I were to wake
I would notice
I hadn't left my room
But my mind is a violent sea
And how I escape is to swim into
my dreams
Which sometimes feel
more real
than reality
With eyes closed my vision is clear
The colors bright,
the sound adheres
to my ears
And I float in the water
No longer bothered
By the thoughts
that plague my mind
When I can keep track of time
I try to keep them closed

For as long as I can muster
Because the world with eyes open
Has lost its luster
And the days are too long
While I wait

for the sun
to be gone
Because in my sleep
I can be myself
And not feel the need to weep
I'll live on a cloud
And without doubt
My head will be
cushioned
sorted out
As I dream I feel peace, a release
The water I go into
When the day is at its end
becomes my friend

Kind of Catharsis

It allows a release
Brings some form of peace
A kind of catharsis
To see into darkness
But what if it's only
Temporary, not solely
Good or bad
It's all I have
Poking holes for light
Helps my sense of sight
Tears in a dark cloud
Still exist in a shroud
Caught between
Wanting one thing
And yet another
Remain under cover
Held in the dark
In need of a spark
A flame to ignite
Inner sunlight

Washes me Over

The wave comes crashing down
It overwhelms me
And washes me over
The wave and I might
As well be one and the same
My heart and mind become heavy
with
The weight of all that water
What doesn't fit inside the cavities
Ebbs from my eyes like
Little waves of their own
Raining down from storm clouds
Unmoving in their sockets
They fall with gravity
As does my body
Soaked so deeply in this liquid
Heavy with my own weight
That I've sunk to the bottom
Of a dark ocean
At least somehow
I've learned to breathe underwater
But I've forgotten how to swim
I'll be under this wave until
I can learn it again

I

Inner sunlight fades
Sun sets without moon rising
Absence is darkness

The Plant Knows

Do you think the plant knows
what it's doing is hard?
To grow and turn into
what it is supposed to be
To start as a seed and feed from
the sun in order to become the
whole of itself
Surviving dark clouds that loom
loud and heavy
Turning tears of rain
into a source from which it gains
the power to bloom
I can only assume the plant takes
the time and effort
because it has to
No other future is possible,
nothing else will do
So like the plant I now reach
toward the sun
Feeling its warmth I begin to open
and coexist with the things from
which I can no longer run
Growing from what has happened
to what will be
Inevitably it is not easy but it was
never supposed to be that way
To remain the same may be easier
but it's a slow decay

So I choose going through the
pain, to break through earth, to
know the hurt
so I can move beyond
And even though I create my own
rain the feeling is worth it because
I'm doing what needs to be done
for me to blossom
And I too like the plant can live as
I am meant to be, wholly
Do you think the plant knows
I look up to it, even though it's
smaller than me?

In the Light

Waking up each morning
Pieces of my skin stick
to my sheets
Flesh unbound, pulling away
A viscous, visceral stretch in the
direction of my movement, a line
between what was and what is
I start each day
Molting, shedding off what
I used to be
Attempting to be comfortable in
my own skin as I begin
To try and determine what's
underneath and let my petals open
To feel a sense of release
From all that I've surrounded
myself in
Trying to grow and get out
from under
What I've been telling myself
was peace
But all along I've been in a war
with the one person I can no
longer ignore
So I do my best to break through
layers and levels of thick
fluid and blood
Painful with the hurt of having a

beating, bleeding heart, I start
With my two red-stained hands
And rip the dead, unwanted
skin off me
So I can not be so
down and heavy
Under the morning sun I have
begun to realize that for which I
strive is to feel completely, openly,
honestly, deeply alive
To have each flower that makes up
who I am blossom and thrive
I'll spend every day peeling away
and clawing through the barriers
I've built up that are in my path
Until all that's left is
pure and right
And I'll wake in the morning
Whole, intact
Blooming in the light

Do I

Matter
Solid   liquid   gas

I am
solid
        liquid
                gas
but do I
                matter?

Being

I've been buried underneath
something for such a long time
A force so strong I've heard it in
practically every rhyme
I've ever written
Bitten
by its teeth, so long and sharp
It grabbed a hold of me
by my heart
Almost from the start
And for years and years
I have been its captive
Trying to dig out and be loud
It hasn't been enough
But now I'm on the cusp
of taking it down
instead of the other way around
Because I know now
It has a name
And it is Shame
And all this time it's controlled
the game
Entangled, intertwined in every
aspect of my being
Controlling the narrative
Of how I've felt I'm supposed
to live
But now that I see it clearly for
what it is and know it by name
I can take steps to move through
it, beyond it, and not continue to
be the same
And perhaps one day Shame
will have no place in this space
that is my body, mind, and heart
Shame will no longer be
something in which I am a part
Because I'll just be me
Being, living gloriously

Challenge

I challenged myself
to write a poem
without a rhyme scheme
which is hard
because
that's all I really do
is rhyme words
with each other
but I've made it to this point
so I'll stop
        while I'm ahead

And Even Then

Sometimes it feels   as if
My heart   is too big for my chest
That it contains
     too many feelings
     too much ache
     and too much love
For such a small cavity
and so the only release
the only means of reprieve
for the heaviness it brings
     Is through my eyes
And even then
Sometimes
     it's too much for them

Wolves

Like the omega in a pack
Prone to disregard
To reject and ignore
I put myself last

Coming up second best
Constantly a beta
But I never really quit
It's just test after test

Maybe one future day
I'll become an alpha
If I do or don't, either way
My friends will give me stamina

I continue to survive
Because there's one thing
I don't lack
The strength of the wolf
Is in the pack

Skeletons

I'm getting rid of any trace
of skeleton
No remnant of life
behind closet doors any more
What you'll see is
    what you'll get
Because if I'm gonna grow
    I have to show
        myself

What's the point
    of having a heart
    if in order to survive
        it has to hide ?

Seeing

Others cannot see
What I cannot see myself
Eyes start to open

By blinding myself
I blinded everyone else
Truth could not be seen

Eyes fully opened
Adjusting to brightness
Vision and mind clear

Look in the mirror
See something once forgotten
I am seeing me

Silent Alarm

Waiting
With patience
Conscientious
Of the relentless
Ticking of time
That continues to run by
Seen
Just out of the corner
Of my eye
A kind of silent alarm
Sends gears spinning
Amplifies the yearning
That can only be resolved
Through learning
In order to belong
To someone else
I first must belong
To myself
I have to use
My heart and hands
Only then
Will I understand
That I have gifts to give
That no one else can
So to fight the loneliness
I take hold of this
Belief that I consist of
A magic made for love

A reminder to no longer
Sit around
With head down
And instead
Go out and find her

Aftershock

A race against the clock
Initial aftershock
Looking to survive
Keep one eye
On the prize
Focusing down the barrel
Finger poised
Pulls back
Drop 'em down the stairwell
Dead weight
Don't hesitate
Concentrate
Last line of defense
For the resistance
But they keep coming back
Contradicting
The tide of life
Running against
The humanity they lack
Gotta keep fighting
Our lives are worth trying
And then
Opening eyelids
Letting the light in
Take a second
To remember
The dreams we see
When we're asleep

Are just as real
To think otherwise
Would be naive
Because there's only
One reality
So this is a lesson
That our lives are a blessing
And we are not here alone
So don't postpone
Doing what you can
To protect and help each other
With strong hearts
Stay the path
For a better future
We are never done
Because justice for all
Is justice for one

Except a Certain Feeling Stays

I wake up in a sweat
My clothes are damp,
    my skin is wet
Returning from a dream
A life that doesn't belong to me
I can't remember what happened
I try to get back
    but   now   it's   long
forgotten
Except a certain feeling stays
And like deja vu
    It comes again
When I least expect it
I think it's telling me
That my dreams are the same
    as what I perceive
    to be reality
None of it belongs to me
There is no difference
    between when I'm
    asleep and awake
All the same things are at stake
My thoughts
    feelings
    relationships
I just have to live,
    and fully commit
Otherwise I might as well quit

So each day and night
I will try and try to live this life
While keeping in mind
I don't know what I'm doing
    or where I'm going
But I'm too determined
to let myself die
    before
        it's my time

II

Tears come rolling down
Salt stings in still open wounds
Can't seem to stay dry

A Call

If the state of the nation
Isn't making you angry or anxious
Are you paying attention
Is your privilege a cover
Used to forget or ignore any other
Because it's not worth the trouble
People are dying in the streets
Forced to their knees
Trying to convince you that they
bleed the same as you do
All of this violence
Surrounded by swallowed
systemic silence
Is anything but righteous
It is oppression
Used as a deadly weapon
To keep those who threaten the
unequal status quo in check by
forcing them to simultaneously
slow and quick deaths
We have to see
That our diversity
Is a blessing from sea
to shining sea
And with clasped hands
We must understand
That this land was built on the
backs of those who have been
made to try to pull themselves up
by their breaking boot straps
If we ever hope to heal
First we need to acknowledge
and reveal
That the unjust state we live in is
all too real
And come together
To thoroughly sever
All the corrupt tethers that keep
us
from moving beyond
We must educate
And peacefully retaliate
To no longer perpetuate a system
that favors only a few
There is so much misplaced fear
But let me be clear
Diversity and differences are here
to excite us with vibrancy and
color like no other
It is a continuous fight
A stand for what is
undeniably right
And until the light goes out in my
eyes I will pursue a more equal
and just world
like the one in my dreams
Will you join me?

Womb

Perhaps   it comes from a past
that was once ours
         But   is now semi-forgotten
A dream we know we had
but
can't quite remember
Something which created a
connection
that was physically cut
        Yet remains between us
An invisible diamond thread
that can
bring us   so close
   while still cutting our hands
Once stained it carries new weight
And it's up to us to not let it slip
away
It becomes harder to hold
   but if we succeed
in keeping it in our grasp
   Its worth becomes more

To Feel the Rhythm of the Earth

is it a gift or a curse
to feel the rhythm of the earth
to know its timing as it turns
keeping track of the count
with each and every sound
I guess it's just the way that I
perceive and process life
so I'll take it as a blessing
even when it keeps me up at night
because it's one of the only things
that helps me feel alive
feeling its force and going berserk
so I'll carry and hold it with pride
it will always be there shining
as a fire inside
allowing me to do what I can
by connecting
my heart and my hands
so with every feel
I can make the beats in my dreams
just as real

Walking Gardens

Diversity is
as old as the earth
and I have to come to understand
that what it's worth
Is everything
The unique differences
in all of us
are what make us glorious
They started growing from the
beginning
in the first garden
to where we are now
The beauty in each of us
compounds
With each breath we take
Each new sun and moon we face
Our diverseness
shows through flora
that grows from us
We are walking gardens
Living, breathing,
connection giving and receiving

Vessels of what is real, good,
and pure
But in order for us to
deeply feel and cure
that which ails us
we must acknowledge
That life blooms
in kaleidoscopic variance
The magnitude of colors, shapes,
and sizes
is there for us to realize
that uniqueness and difference
Are radiant
The fact that my garden
is not the same as yours
should make us want to explore
each other
The fact that your garden
is different from mine
Makes me smile and come alive
When I use my blooming eyes
to look at my reflection

I see my garden
with a perception
that wants to care for and tend to
What I am made of
And when I use those same eyes
to see what's blossoming from you
I will care, tend, feel, help
All of the above
to have us both bloom and grow
Because this I know
Your garden and my garden
are arrays of life never seen before
and will never be seen again
So to that end
I will defend, cherish, and love
both our gardens
Magnificently dissimilar
And make sure
we shine loud and bright
and proud
Until my flowers
take their final bow

State

The state of my existence
is not up for debate
My heart is pure and loud
and it drowns out all your hate
The strength of my heart
pumps into my fists
I'll fight your hate with love
each and every day
You'll know I mean it
through bloody knuckles
and a smile
Red with the blood from my heart
There is no other way
Shining proudly through my eyes
Glory and fury, a berserker for life
Intense and held deep within
You won't question the lion
Feel it when I tell you
I am here to stay

Steps

Sometimes the world feels so big
a macrocosm
within which I am but a breath
    that lasts for a nanosecond
But within me
a paradox resides
because even though
I am so micro
My heart
is vast and infinite
And there are days
when I come to
        the edge
of my personal Penrose staircase
and don't know what to do
with all I carry in my chest
Because it's the same size
as the world
I take a   step
into it all
It's like I become one
with the   infinite abyss
               and begin   to exist

III

The clouds open up
Lightning comes and I'm hoping
To hold it in hand

For my

Unbound
How do I sound now?
I am the same
but simultaneously not somehow
Instead of playing the same game
that had me buried for days
and years   and years
on end
I decided to defend   myself
For my past self
The child I still hold inside

For my present self
Who just wants to find purpose
and place in life

For my future self
A being yet unknown who will
have grown
from past and present seeds sown

I am unbound
And the farther I go
the more I am who I'm
meant to be
I am more
honest, real, and fully
committed to living with

a pure heart
I will never be done
Not with growing, learning,
and being unbound

My song is still being sung
But now I have solid ground
from which I can start

Body

We start as bodies
A vessel to hold our infinite being
To hold our truth and love
To know this is to understand that
We are more than just bodies
And bodies are reflections
of what's inside
A body is beautiful because
The soul inside it is beautiful
A body is strong because
The person who moves it is strong
A body exists so we may connect
in a physical way that equates
to our connection in the unseen
plane
To reduce someone solely
to their physical appearance
is to ignore them
To dehumanize them
To attempt to make them so small
they aren't worth your
slightest consideration
Because in the grand scheme
a body is a minuscule portion
of what makes us who we are
We are light
We are sound
We are love

And those things are endless and
cannot be confined to a body
But it's easier to other and hate
if the body becomes the focus and
we reduce people to
physical arbitrary attributes
So let us celebrate our bodies
and our selves
Not for their physicality
or appearance
But for their capacity to
hold and carry
Our resilience
Our compassion
Our infinite being

Carpe

It takes heart
to start
Again and again
Each and every day
There is no end
There's just life
it's rife
with complications
Ups
Downs
Turn arounds
Taken in
as information
to be processed
Synthesized
Wheels turning
in the mind
Hoping that someone else
Feels
Thinks
Believes
Like yourself
So maybe you'll give them
a piece from deep inside
Then they'll do the same
Won't hesitate
and you'll both listen
to what's within

Knowing
The love you have
and share
is rich and rare
Purifies
The darkness
of the outside
two Hearts
with all their
might
carpe diem
carpe noctum
They'll greet
the moon and
sun
each time they come
Together
As one

IV

Open connection
Warmth from one to another
Inner sunlight grows

Weather Report

Depression

I am a weeping willow who droops
so low I may as well be one with
the ground

Anger

I am a carnivorous plant who
wants to bite into all that crosses
its path

Love

I am the softest lamb's ear who
will give you all the comfort and
support you need

Rose-colored

I see Love
Through rose-colored glasses
So warm and bright
Like rays of light
Form the sunrise
Illuminating what's around
In various pink tones
For everyone else
But when it comes to myself
That hue goes away
And becomes blank
Like an absence of recall
About a dream
That took its toll
How do I learn
To make it stay ?

Syndrome

On the days
when I feel
      good
outside the realm
of my usual
      depression
It is as if
I am
      an
            imposter

Beacon

I wish to be
a beacon

your beacon

a light
           to guide you
           to give you
somewhere   to go
somewhere   to be

but it seems
I am only
surrounded by the dark
as there is

           no one at sea

V

I sleep and wonder
Dream of a past life now dark
Hope for bright future

Mother

An ode to
The grand Mother
And in turn
All mothers
You give us life
That can only
Be described
With words that
Won't do you justice
The majesty
Of your gifts
That flow through
Earth and fire
Air and water
And all of us
Spawn love
And so I thank you

Gold scars

The scales I've been holding with
my hand oscillate between being
tipped one way or the other,
there's no middle ground,
no happy medium,
akin to magnets that repel when
too close together
At times my one free hand is
pulled by the heavier side, it rises
up and hits my head, but not to
my surprise, the sensation caused
offers a temporary release but
once I unclench my fist the scales
dispute so there goes the relief
I can't keep it at a distance
because I'm the one holding it,
and keeping it at arm's length
is like dealing with the devil, it's all
just one big trick
I'm getting stronger holding the
weight, maybe that's something I
can be proud of, one good thing to
take away from all of this, while I
continue to swing back and forth,
hands that drip blood from up
above
Gold scars across my hand racing
up around my arm, soon I won't

separate from so called justice,
smash the glass,
ring the alarm
It returns to my heart, the place
from which it all starts,
The metronome controls which
way the scales go,
in my own time signature,
I create a new future

Find me

Come find me
on the floor of my room
Tangled in the
        middle
of my heartstrings
I want you to tug
        and touch them all
Make your way
In   between   them
toward where I lay
As you pull each one
I can hear the music
        you bring out in me
Please continue
Traveling   deeper
      into my space
          And unravel me

Fell/Fall

Ever since I was a child so young
I fell in love with
      the idea of falling in love
So much so that I put it
      Above   all else
And now that years have passed
The seed of loving love I planted
is still unmatched
Yet I don't know if I fully grasp
      what love is
Life is a constant of cycles
And loving love can feel like a
series of trials
But my love for love I can't deny
      even though
I'm not sure if I'll ever
      Truly   hold it

VI

Tonight I will dream
An optical illusion
Called reality

Unfold to Become

A flower weighed down
By the heft of darkness
Cannot truly bloom

My petals have shrunk
Lack of sunlight and belief
Start to grow again

I'm opening up
My petals reach out for light
Unfold to become

Petals born anew
Trying hard to blossom now
Out from under dark

My garden will keep
And continue to blossom
I'll forever grow

I'm becoming me
Flower with inner sunrise
Watch me while I bloom

Still Just as Real

I wake up with bruises
And I don't know how they get
there
Like they're self-inflicted in my
sleep
Can't escape myself even in
dreams

Ignoring what's deep inside
In a perverted form of self-defense
Waiting for night to feel alive in a
dream
But it makes no difference

I try not to get overwhelmed
Between dreaming and being
awake
To take a breath and self-reflect
I realize my heart is at stake

REM sleep won't save me
Dreams are just another form of
life
Something which I can't rely on
Even though I try and try

If it's all in my heart
It's still just as real
Believing is living
And I believe what I feel

Anchor

If one little thing goes wrong
It throws me so off track
   I get so far from   myself
Like there's no coming back

Overwhelmed
      by such small things
Hyper sensitivity
Try to keep sight of the shore
So I don't lose   myself at sea

But while my head's eating circles
It gives me time to ponder
And realize land won't save me
      The shore's not my savior

I come to conclude
      that   there's   nothing
wrong
with being adrift in the ocean
      as long as I understand
How to navigate inner commotion
So while my heart still beats
     I listen to its fervor
     and comprehend
I have to be
    my own anchor

So for once
      I'll do myself a favor
      And be my own anchor

Now the ocean and me
Get along gloriously

Internal rhythm gets stronger
Because
      I'm my own anchor

Blood Red Godsend

It rises up
from below to above
A mosh pit shove
and swing of arms
Sound the alarm
So loud it swallows every other
sound
Glorious fury
Astounds all who surround
But within there is peace
a kind of ease
Heartbeat
Steady as a metronome
with a hidden pride
atop its throne
Kinetic energy
waiting to be released
Venus fly trap
wanting something
to enter its path
To hold and crush
Power
to devour
Pitcher plant
Drawing you in
and so begins
Decay
With which to play

a song of love and rage
If the sticks break
switch to fists
Blood red
Godsend
A loyal heart
that of a lion
Sharp teeth
that spell danger
for those who see the smile
Pure nature
Berserker
Say your prayers
No compromise
Come out
on the other side
So alive

Born

I was born in the midst of change
A reawakening from cold and dark
Towards the spark of spring
When what the sun and wind
bring
Is furious growth and possibility
       And out came   me
In the midst of it all
Sprouting with my surroundings
The flowers took me in
They taught me glorious lessons
To listen to my metronome
And share what was given
Hoping to form heartfelt
connection
Between myself and others
With pride   loyalty
and love
How to access my pure nature
And let it be
As familiar as my shadow
    I'm a born dandelion kicker

Sun/Moon

Born swimming
with the sun
Roaring
with the moon
I came out
of the womb
A wildflower
Wild child
Not in body
or action
But in heart
and in mind
Endowed with
an imagination
That helped fight
the alienation
The way
I remained
Loyal to me
was to leave
this reality
And enter another
Alone
my dreams
would come alive
And I felt right
At home
in a place

I couldn't show
to anyone else
Because God forbid
they see my real self
But if I was created
by a supreme deity
Perhaps maybe
The song
I play
isn't wrong
It's tuned perfectly
to my key
And the beat
is in rhythm
with my metronome
that was gifted
to me at birth
And now feels
like my home
Because I'm living
fully in it
As me
Simply and purely

Blessed be

Blessed be our scars and marks
Each constellation upon our
bodies
I will cherish and behold the glory
of every single star
Recognizing patterns that are
housed between our arms
Connecting the dots of treasure
maps that lead to determined
hearts
It's in our nature to express our
fury through God-given art
Drawn from blood and flesh that
keep us from coming apart
Reflections of the five senses and
illustrations so pure of what it
takes to make it this far
Physical manifestations to be seen
and touched while others are
held by hands only opening to be
heartfelt when accessed by a true
counterpart
Blessed be the marks and scars
that make us who we are

All I Ask

I want to feel

the sun on my skin
and dig into the dirt
For I am made
of the same salt as the Earth

the water from the sea
learning from
the push and pull
because it too flows in me

Love on my lips
a bridge between hearts
so a life together can begin

All I ask
Is hold nothing back

Music

I am sheets of notes
Scribbled onto paper
By rhythmic hands
I am a metronome
Keeping time
Through pulses of blood
I am drums and cymbals
Working together
To exemplify my feelings
I am music
Hoping to be heard

Landscape

On days like these
When everything feels
     so apart from   me
This loneliness
Effect of our common
circumstance
We talk through
     invisible wires
About all that transpires
But it lacks a certain intimacy
Intense separation
Along and coming undone
And try as I might
To put up a fight
The space between
gets the better of me
The distance   does its
damage
My bleeding heart hemorrhages
It comes out clear through my
eyes
Adds salt to my wounds
I fill up with an ocean inside of
me
     And sink to the floor
Always wanting more
I'll be your anchor if you'll have
me

Once the sun has gone away
And the moon takes its place
The wa(e)i(gh)t is just too much
for me to take
A slight reprieve
While I dream
But I go to sleep knowing
     It starts again
tomorrow morning

After Effect

Craving connection
But it seems
I've forgotten
My social skills
Have become rotten
I no longer know
How to approach someone
With confidence to show
Who I am
Any sort of plan
Slips through my hands
Like trying to catch rain
And so I just abstain
But deep down
I crave and crave
So I'll have to relearn
How to be brave
And vulnerable
To open up to another
With hope and wonder
That they will accept me
And together
We can be
      Friends

VII

I will spill my guts
To those who matter most
And not feel empty

Get the Symphony Going

Dandelion kicker
The fire within
Never flickers
Quicker and quicker
It grows
Burning strong
Born on the cusp
Of spring
Sound rings
Harmony
With the flowers
Around me
Creating a melody
My heart beats to
Nothing else to do
But give in
To my pure nature
A berserker
Feeling it all
So completely deeply
I become
The music
I am made of
Loyal and loud
Furious and proud
Giving me
The opportunity
For glory

To seek something holy
Spreading love
That comes
From within and above
So others too
Can be
The maestro
Of their own symphony

Looking up

Next time
You feel like
The only way through
Is a fist to your head side
Think about
The child
That is still alive
And try to become
On whom they can rely
Because they carry a light
Deep down inside
And it still resides
Within you now
So show them how
To be proud
It's not with inward punches
That dim the light down
The darkness
Can only be fought
By overcoming
What has been self-taught
Fight for the child
Not against them
And fight for yourself
Use your hands
To understand and illuminate
All the glory
You were meant to create

Put to use
Your love and rage
Your heart will be the metronome
For great things to come
So next time
You feel the desire
To take a swing
At your own being
Remember the kid
Who's counting on you
To be the one
They can look up to

Trance

I take all I feel
And put it into words
On paper
In hopes that it will reveal
Perhaps express
Something important
Or hidden
That no longer
Is to be concealed
And into beats
Through the help of sticks
and instruments
Leaving traces of myself
Loyal and proud
Lion-hearted and loud
In red
In and on my skin
And the drum heads
My emotions
So embedded within me
That even when I sleep
They remain awake
And force their way
Into my dreams
Creating new reality
They put me in a trance
So glorious
I become my pure nature

Suffice it to say
I can't and won't
Live any other way
Berserkergang

Self-taught

There is a ring
Encircling me
its size ebbs and flows
with how much hurt
I have been   overthrown by
The tighter it gets
            the less I let people in
and I leave   this place
to go live amongst the stars
because the wounds I've received
haven't yet turned into scars
And the ring will remain
            to disrupt my circulation
until I come back
            down to the earthly plane
for cardiac restoration
Time and space
are the only instruments
            at my disposal
Loosening the ring   slowly
as I eventually stitch
            my heart back together
a self-taught heart surgeon

Armor

Being clear, honest
A flower starts to open
Makes space for what's true

Tender to the touch
But going deep with strong roots
Feeling more secure

Heart planted in hands
Held with care, beating steady
Continues to grow

Surrounded by sun
Petals cover with color
So bright and lightweight

Pulse getting louder
Safe within the heartfelt truth
Will bloom resilient

Vulnerability
Such powerful protection
Soft petals, strong shield

Left Waiting

I had my arms out in front
Palms facing up
Holding a heart
But it was not enough
You took a bite
Held it in your teeth
I was marked with a scar
And left waiting for yours

Morning Person

I think that I'm a morning person
until the nights when I don't want
to go to sleep
I find things to occupy the time
between the sunset and my
dreams
I know that once I close my eyes
I'll be so far from here and I won't
want to return again
Have the darkness take me and let
me disappear

I wake up in a sweat so cold with
water from another place
My eyes open reluctantly with
water of their own to mourn a
nonexistent space

I think that I'm a morning person
until the nights when I don't want
to go to sleep
I find ways to pass the time
between the sunset and my
dreams
I know it's part of an elusive goal
to feel like I can have the illusion
of control
Have my hands entwined with

those of time so I shape the day
instead of any other way

I think that I'm a morning person
until the nights when I don't want
to go to sleep
I find ways to spend the time
between the sunset and my
dreams
The effort that it takes correlates
to how long I've been away from
my bed
Using every drop of energy to
push through the sorrow and the
stalling begins knowing I'll have
to
do it again tomorrow

Scar my eyes to trick myself into
living outside the constructs of
time
That way I can't tell when it's
sunrise or sunset
And the light and the dark will
make no difference

VIII

I exist between
Neither one nor the other
And yet am still both

Signal

Attempt to reconnect
A signal forgotten that got lost on
its way from heart to head
But the wires remain and repeat a
cold refrain
A message corrupted by
neural demons
And so rose a darkness from which
they could feed on
Now in a waking dream I dive
into my stream of consciousness
       There's a child waiting for
me among disconnected electricity
Sitting next to them I hold out my
hand and extend whatever pulse
I have
Giving all the light I can to
illuminate the fading sun within
We become one as it's what should
have always been
And how it's really been all along
       Because the child is me
So the signal is regained
A mutual spark between two
heads and hearts that are now
fused together
As one they will never sever
The sun inside begins to rise and

the warmth I'm feeling aids
in healing
and the hungry demons who've
been feeding on inner turmoil
       Will turn into gargoyles

Of my own

I know there's a possibility that I
could be the villain in
someone's story
Just want it to not be that
of my own
After all this time, hoping to have
grown with the seeds I've sown
Trying my best to find a little
peace of mind in my own time
Catalyst caused the spark, shown a
light in all that dark while making
such a deep mark
Leaves a scar for me to see
Helps my vision to be free from all
the dark debris
Lifts a weight right off my heart
Its beating can now restart, as I'm
no longer coming apart
Intact and feeling whole
The sun can now reach my soul
And while I take in its light,
I know I no longer need to fight
The darkness fades away and the
clouds are white not gray
Knowing it's not the end but
rather a place to begin, I can be a
better friend

So with my heartbeat as my
metronome, I begin to
find my home

Sensing

All this time with everything kept
inside
Daydreams that seem more real
although they are forced to be
concealed
Percussive shadows in the dark
hoping for a light to create a spark
Wanting to be heard and seen not
just in the dreams of a singular
being
To connect with another through
a unique language
And know what the feeling of
warmth is
Unknown when it will begin
Conducted by lightning shot
down
from the sky
Striking two, not twice, at the
same time
Electricity pulses to my hands
and unplanned they spill my guts
sensing trust
My hands are holding flowers to
be given that come from within
Colored red and beating from my
heart
I am open and willing to start

Next

Words that mean one thing
Can turn into something
Between sets of ears
What makes it real
Which is the answer
To the question being posed
Does it have one
If neither mind knows
How long does it take
For the translation to take place
Please don't misunderstand
These words are all
I have to command
But are they necessary and needed
Their forms and sounds
Can be so fleeting
Remember the feelings
That came along with them
Those will last longer
Do they even have an end
Confused by shapes and lines
I don't know how many times
I've tried to tell myself
I'm doing fine
But those are just simple words
Like all the others
And I'm wondering when
I'll be able to recover
Because it's complex

In excess
Like everything is
But this is something else
And I don't know what to do
All I can do is tell you
Hope the sentiment isn't lost
Reveal what's deep down
No matter the cost
Trust it isn't fake
It's not a mistake
Follow the sound
From ears to hearts
We speak the same tongue
Breathe it in
Through our lungs
We're living this
It does exist
The question is
What comes next?

IX

The sky rages loud
Sound of the thunder clapping
Booms from inside me

Part IV

I've learned that who I'm meant
to be doesn't make living easy
But it's what makes me real
All I know for certain is how and
what I feel
So I carry it with honor between
my shoulders
The deep red badge of a berserker

I didn't choose to have this kind
of
heart
It was gifted to me at birth
And now I understand how much
it's worth
It means everything to me
So I keep it well protected
in the middle of my body
If you look closely enough you
can
see it between my shoulders
The deep red badge of a berserker

As I bleed alive
I smile deep inside
I'll leave my true mark on this
earth
And go berserk

I listen to my heart
Its rhythm beats loud and strong
And gives me focus and purpose
In the fury of a glorious trance
Determined in a heartfelt stance
This badge will never leave me

And I'll hold it inside and make it
shine
With loyalty and pride
I give in to fully live and my pure
nature takes over
I'm a berserker

Found only when I'm dreaming

Wanting what I see
Found only when I'm dreaming
No need to return

Wanting what I see
Found only when I'm dreaming
I just want to stay

Wanting what I see
Found only when I'm dreaming
Please don't make me go

Wanting what I see
Found only when I'm dreaming
Will I make it real

Atop a Throne

King with a crown
Sitting
      atop a
            throne
      Alone
Holding out   hope
Amidst the sound
      And silence
Of a broken   heart

X

The thunder's hands clap
Soothes what's in my lion heart
Physical echoes

Flowers at my Feet

I spent so long
With my head down
    Looking only at the
Flowers at my feet
Not realizing
I was stifling   the growth
Of those within me
I didn't understand
That the flowers at my soles
Were produced by my energy
    And if I could just focus
With the beat of my heart
The internal garden
    would bloom   in me

A patterned garden
I won't let it be my   end
It'll be my rebirth instead
A place for my heart and head

My life is in my own
heart and hands
Recognize the pattern and see
It reflects what I carry
    inside of me
Flowers that create
    a maze   only I
have the map
    to get through

A Rush of Blood and Sound

I always talk about fighting for
love
With words and hands I try my
best for what truly matters
But it seems I'm the one I combat
with the most as two fists pound
against my skull
Is it really so unhealthy if it's just
in my nature
The percussion I create does me a
Favor

It gives me a rush of blood and
sound
There's something pure about it
in the end
A catch and release of all the
things that swim up from my
heart to my head
All of it is transient as it never
lasts forever but that doesn't seem
to matter as it's always just around
the corner

I can go to battle so easily for
anyone else
But it's like my heart stops
bleeding when it comes to myself
And the red only pours from

cracked knuckles between
throwing punches at demons that
come from inside of me

With each punch I throw
Shadow boxing with live shades
of black
I'm in the trance of a berserker
My fists greet the demons with a
distinct kind of fervor
I give it my all with glorious fury
To be loyal to my heart
The demons become my
counterparts
Absorbing through my skin
They reform within and I begin
Now I'm someone more
Won't be the same as before

Paradox

Both/and is the truth
Paradoxical pursuit
Life's in the middle

No more black and white
Loyal to the mystery
Unknown and alive

Amongst the between
Search for questions and answers
Belief in the gray

Liberation is
Living in what we don't know
And calling it home

XI

Repetition is
A pattern recognition
Learn from deja vu

Aren't I

Life is for the living
Purgatory is for the waiting dead
And without love
Hell is the thing you create inside
your head

So I'll live by my heart
To forgo being torn between the
dying and the rest
And I'll remind myself
Love is the one thing that's always
          right
I'll fight for love with heart and
fists
Because I'm alive, aren't I?

Looking to Take Shape

I want the ocean to swallow me
Leave no trace, there's no
returning
No one will remember the day
When I let the water sweep me
under
It's better off this way

I can't think of anything better
Waves take me with their temper
It matches these feelings of mine
Swirling wild with outer forces
And crashing loud inside

There's lightning in my mind
It touches down on water that
swells beneath my skin
The shock it makes can stop the
flow of time
But I'm not sure if it's good or
bad, will help me lose or win

I'm nothing more than water
Looking to take shape
Making noise and trying to relate
But I can't seem to find my place

XII

The sun, with kindness
Lends me its warmth and its light
Replenishing force

English Lesson

Small
>   Adjective
describing how I can feel
when depression gets
the better of me

Fold
>   Verb
the action I take upon myself
as I melt into the floor
and my body exists no more

Darkly
>   Adverb
how I think and speak
my sense of self becoming
more and more weak

Me
>   Noun
tasked with reforming all that
makes me up
unsure if it's something
I'm capable of

But I might as well try and see
what becomes of it
because I
>   won't be the death of me

Romantic

a romantic
      withstanding`
Crowned King
of the hopeless
      bleeding
            hearts on sleeves

In/Visible

Am I invisible
Not in my form
       I take up physical space
       shy and testing the water
       full   of   anticipatory
anxiety
       never   diving   in   too
quickly
       delicate and holding back
       my cacophony of waves
But in who I am
       a shadow symphony
       rhythmic din
       of water, light, and heart
       swimming with love
       in an ocean of sun
       comfortable in the sounds
       of emotional exuberance
Will I ever be seen
Visible
       as me   ?

Out/Through

I had been buried alive
So deep in the dirt
The dark was my friend
All I knew was the hurt

I was dead weight
Stuck under my own shadow
I had put myself there
With the help of those I followed

As I was lying in the ground
I came to understand
The only living future
Was the one held in my hands

With my knuckles and will
I fought my way out so the sun I
could view
I could feel my rhythm growing
louder
Now I can find the answers to my
questions
Because the only true way out is
Through

Realize that time is mine only if I
take the strides to move through
all the lies and make myself my
home

There is no greater force than my
internal metronome
And everything it stands for is
protected by the hardest fists and
sharpest teeth
You have no chance because its
love and fury never sleeps

Watercolor Eyes

The music sometimes stops but
       my rhythm never does
Punches might not be thrown
       but my fists remain closed
Hold my heart in my hands
       hope you can understand
The fighting can recede
       but the pain never leaves
Reaching for something to hold on
tight to keep me fully in this life
Looking at the world through
watercolor eyes
I don't know how else to exist
I go berserk when I'm purely alive

The Best Kind of View

Music reaches in
grabs your heart
and with all the pulsations
        and rhythmic vibrations
puts forth
all that you feel
makes it tangible to your ears
overcome by its swell
you can see yourself
        echoing back to you
and the lyrical landscape
you now exist in
        is the best kind of view

Penrose

I walk around
my own personal staircase
of Penrose name
Looking for the ledge
       the loop continues instead

I know one day
I'll end up where I want
There's no destination
it's about understanding
       there was never a landing

The Penrose steps
I walk everyday
It's just a matter of time
       before I step off the edge
Go berserk in the descent
As my pure self

When I walk off the steps
and begin to go through
It's the only way out
       Become who I was meant
to

A leap   of faith
because the only way   forward
       is without the staircase

In the abyss
I transform what is
Begin to exist
Dove and fist

XIII

To grow and evolve
Inevitable striving
Becoming one's self

In the Details

Don't think
Don't even blink
The clock only goes one way
Tick tick tick
The present becomes the past
It never really lasts
And what's ahead
Is merely an extension
Of the time that's already slipping
Through your hands
Nothing ever really goes to plan
God laughs
In the aftermath
And the only hope
You can hope to have
Is to become one
With the sun, the moon, the truth
Nowhere left to hide
Let out a roar
Never heard before
The devil's in the details
Flying fists
Pointed horns
Sharp teeth and winged feet
You are becoming more
Gifted with love and fury
Feelings as big as waves
Emotions aplenty

A heart so whole
The loudest metronome
Away with illusion
Be done with confusion
Time has no hold
Over you any longer
Because you're a berserker

Path

I will not seek what I am
I'll no longer fight who I'm
meant to be
All I ever need is inside of me
Everything I feel I hear in sound
Coming from within
A force so loud
I go berserk to my heartbeat
It keeps me loyal and honest
There's no other way
For me to truly exist
The bleeding muscle in my chest
Is my strongest body part
More powerful than the rest
Understanding now that all
I feel is real
On my way with fury toward glory
What's inside myself
is where to start
The path I have chosen
Is only for the pure of heart